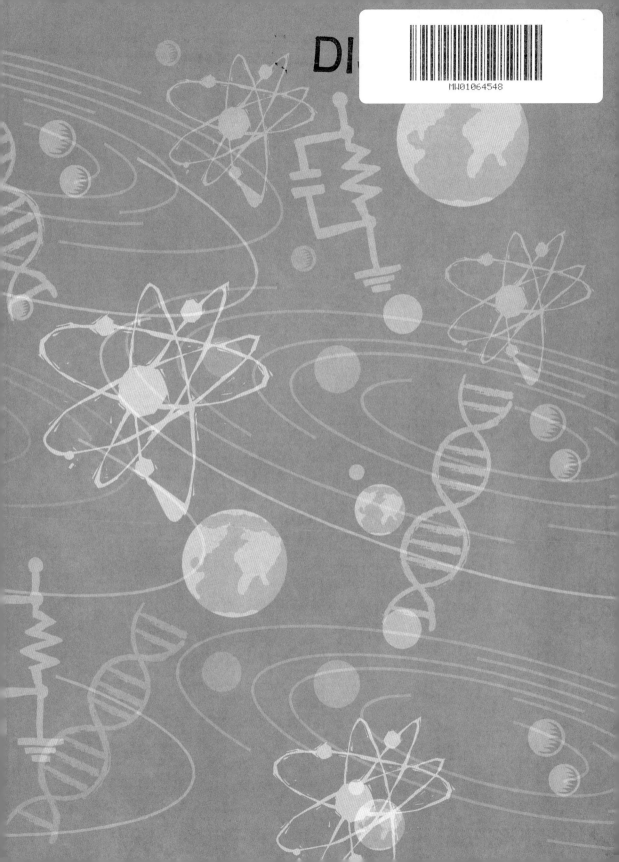

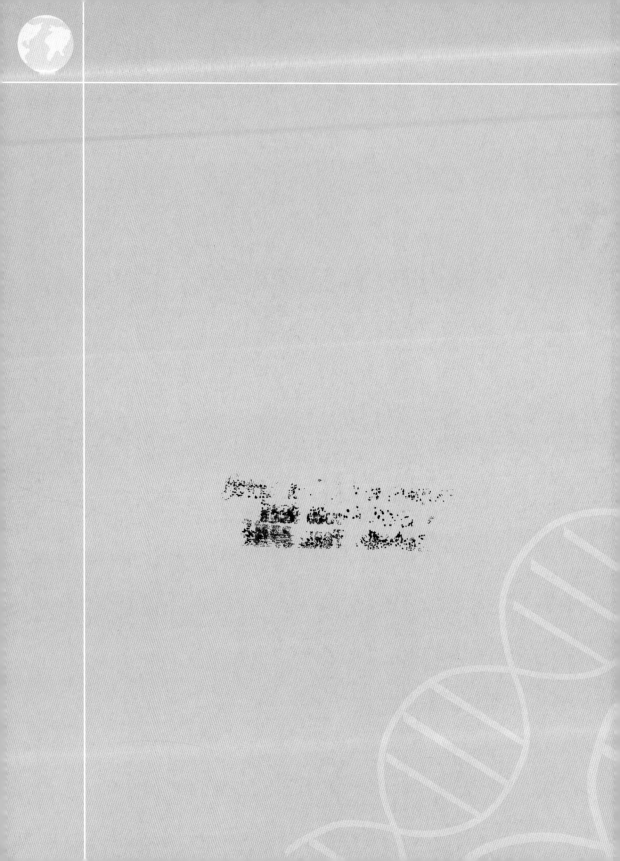

Louis Pasteur:

Founder of Microbiology

by Lisa Zamosky

MISSION: SCIENCE

Science Contributor
Sally Ride Science
Science Consultants
Thomas R. Ciccone, Science Educator
Ronald Edwards, Science Educator

MISSION:

Developed with contributions from Sally Ride Science™

Sally Ride
Science

Sally Ride Science™ is an innovative content company dedicated to fueling young people's interests in science.

Our publications and programs provide opportunities for students and teachers to explore the captivating world of science—from astrobiology to zoology.

We bring science to life and show young people that science is creative, collaborative, fascinating, and fun.

To learn more, visit www.SallyRideScience.com

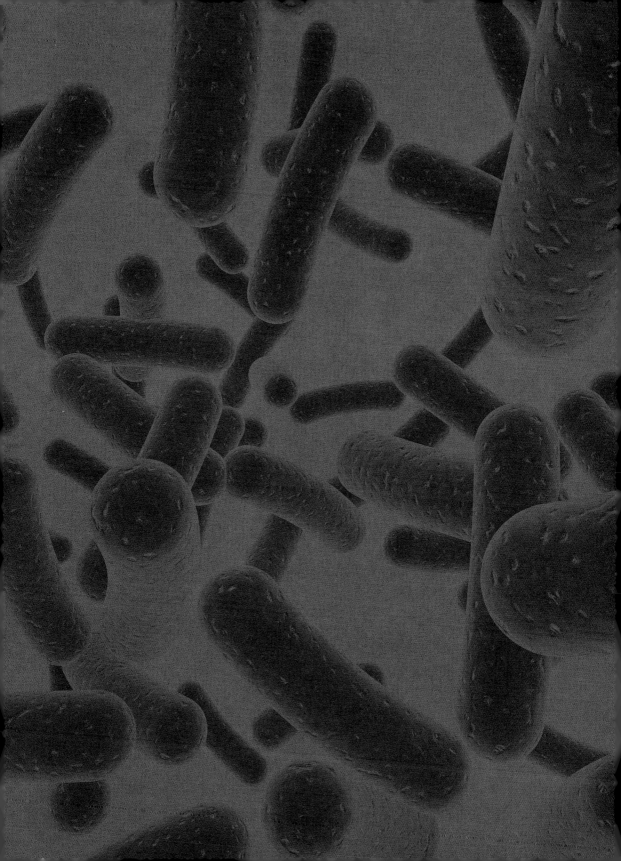

First hardcover edition published in 2009 by
Compass Point Books
151 Good Counsel Drive
P.O. Box 669
Mankato, MN 56002-0669

Editor: Brenda Haugen
Designer: Heidi Thompson
Editorial Contributor: Sue Vander Hook

Art Director: LuAnn Ascheman-Adams
Creative Director: Keith Griffin
Editorial Director: Nick Healy
Managing Editor: Catherine Neitge

 This book was manufactured with paper containing at least 10 percent post-consumer waste.

Library of Congress Cataloging-in-Publication Data
Zamosky, Lisa.
Louis Pasteur : founder of microbiology / Lisa Zamosky.
     p. cm. — (Mission: Science)
 Includes index.
 ISBN 978-0-7565-3962-7 (library binding)
1. Pasteur, Louis, 1822–1895. 2. Microbiologists—France—Biography—Juvenile literature.
3. Microorganisms—Juvenile literature. 4. Food—Pasteurization—Juvenile literature.
5. Scientists—France—Biography—Juvenile literature. I. Title. II. Series.
QR31.P37Z36 2008
579.092—dc22
[B]   2008007726

Visit Compass Point Books on the Internet at *www.compasspointbooks.com*
or e-mail your request to *custserv@compasspointbooks.com*

Table of Contents

Sheep and cattle were dying all over France. It was the 1870s, and farmers had no idea why their livestock were dropping dead. France's farm economy was in trouble.

French scientist Louis Pasteur believed harmful microorganisms were the cause. But no one believed his so-called germ theory. Even doctors didn't think germs could cause infection or disease. They didn't wash their hands or clean their instruments before operating on patients.

Pasteur didn't let the skeptics stop him. He continued to study and experiment. In 1877, German scientist Heinrich

Louis Pasteur ⬆

Hermann Robert Koch discovered the bacterium that was killing sheep and cattle. The disease was called anthrax. Pasteur went to work to find a way to protect them from this deadly disease. By 1881, he developed a vaccine, but he had to convince the people of France it would work.

Pasteur's vaccine ➡ protected France's sheep and cows from the deadly anthrax virus.

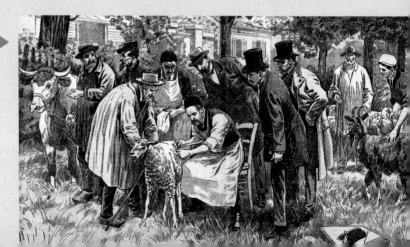

Deadly Anthrax

The bacterium that causes anthrax is called *Bacillus anthracis*. Normally it lives in the soil. Animals that graze on grass and other plants are infected more often than people and other animals.

These bacteria change when they don't have enough food or are exposed to changing temperatures. They form spores that sit dormant, waiting for the right conditions. The spores are deadly. Animals and humans can become infected through open sores or cuts in their skin, by inhaling spores in the air, or by eating infected meat.

Antibiotics can sometimes cure anthrax in its early stages. But the best protection from anthrax is being vaccinated before exposure to the bacteria.

Anthrax has been used as a biological weapon. In 2001, someone purposely sent anthrax spores through the U.S. mail. Five people died, and 22 became ill.

Anthrax is one of the few bacteria that form long-living spores.

In 1882, Pasteur finally had the chance to try out his vaccine. He injected it into 25 healthy sheep; another 25 healthy sheep were not vaccinated. Then Pasteur gave all 50 sheep a deadly dose of anthrax. The 25 vaccinated sheep survived, and the rest died within three days. Pasteur had proved his vaccine worked.

Within two years, vaccinations eliminated anthrax from France's sheep and cattle. Pasteur immediately became a national hero. He would go on to discover much more, including many vaccines that would save millions of lives. And he would go down in history as one of the giants of science.

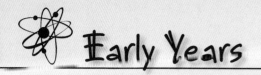

Louis Pasteur was born December 27, 1822, in Dole, France. His family worked as tanners, turning animal hides into leather.

In school, Louis was an average student. He preferred fishing to studying, and his main interest was drawing. He drew many pictures of his family and friends. As a teenager, Louis became a much better student and won many school awards. His headmaster recognized that Louis was very smart and encouraged him to apply to a college in Paris. Very few people were accepted into this college, which trained people to be teachers in the sciences or arts.

At the age of 15, Louis packed his bags and went to Paris. But he was soon too homesick to stay, and his father brought him home. Louis didn't even take the test required to get into the college.

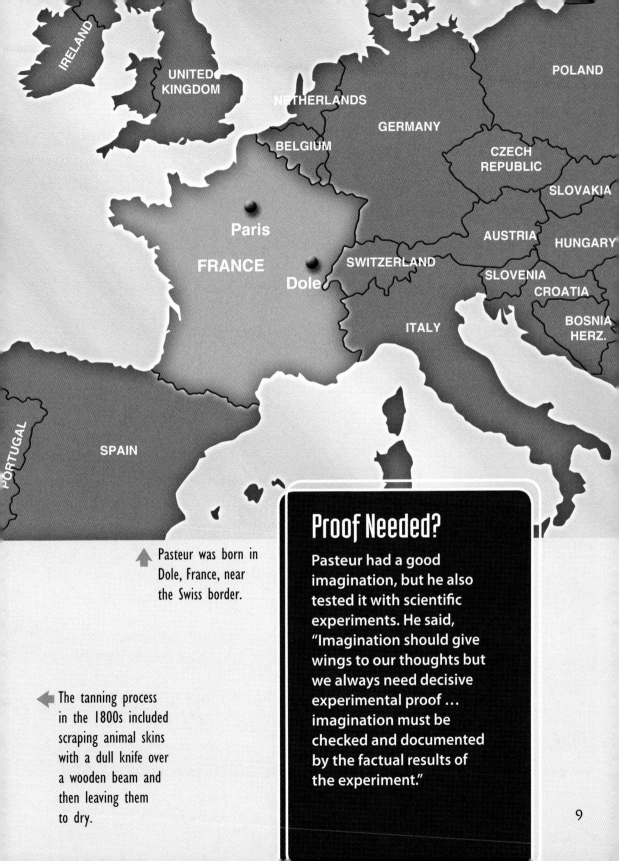

IRELAND

UNITED
KINGDOM

NETHERLANDS

POLAND

GERMANY

BELGIUM

CZECH
REPUBLIC

SLOVAKIA

Paris

AUSTRIA

HUNGARY

FRANCE

SWITZERLAND

SLOVENIA

Dole

CROATIA

BOSNIA
HERZ.

ITALY

PORTUGAL

SPAIN

Pasteur was born in Dole, France, near the Swiss border.

The tanning process in the 1800s included scraping animal skins with a dull knife over a wooden beam and then leaving them to dry.

Proof Needed?

Pasteur had a good imagination, but he also tested it with scientific experiments. He said, "Imagination should give wings to our thoughts but we always need decisive experimental proof … imagination must be checked and documented by the factual results of the experiment."

9

College and Chemistry

When Pasteur returned home from Paris, he enrolled in a college near his home and earned a degree in science. Then he went back to Paris and took the college entrance exam. In 1843, at the age of 21, he was accepted by the École Normale Supérieure and began studying chemistry.

Pasteur worked hard to learn about chemical elements. He was especially interested in the nature of crystals, solids formed by the hardening of chemical elements. His doctoral thesis, a paper required to graduate, was all about crystals.

At the age of 26, Pasteur earned a doctor of science degree. He began teaching chemistry and physics, first in a high school and then at the University of Strasbourg in France. All the while, Pasteur never stopped learning, researching, and conducting scientific experiments.

Testing Himself

Pasteur took the entrance exam twice at the École Normale Supérieure. The first time, he received the 15th highest score. This was good enough to be accepted, but it wasn't good enough for Pasteur. He wanted to do better and didn't enter school until he had scored higher. The second time, he received the fourth highest score.

◀ Pasteur as a young man

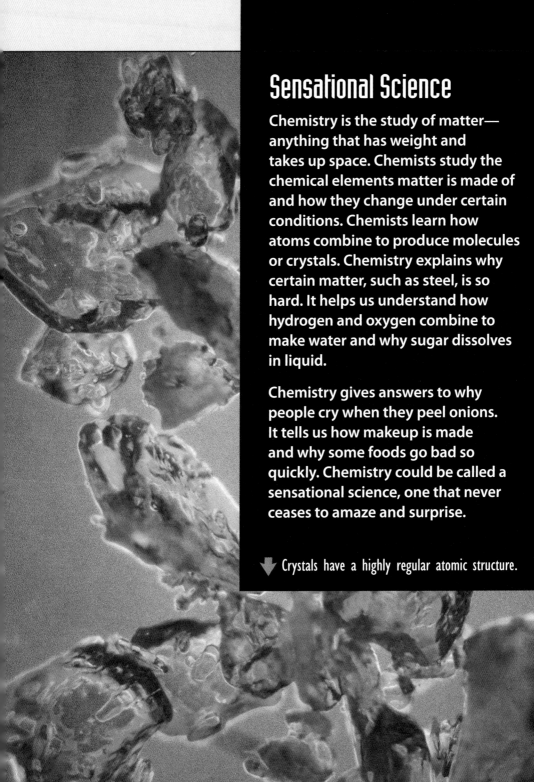

Sensational Science

Chemistry is the study of matter—anything that has weight and takes up space. Chemists study the chemical elements matter is made of and how they change under certain conditions. Chemists learn how atoms combine to produce molecules or crystals. Chemistry explains why certain matter, such as steel, is so hard. It helps us understand how hydrogen and oxygen combine to make water and why sugar dissolves in liquid.

Chemistry gives answers to why people cry when they peel onions. It tells us how makeup is made and why some foods go bad so quickly. Chemistry could be called a sensational science, one that never ceases to amaze and surprise.

Crystals have a highly regular atomic structure.

Louis and Marie Pasteur

While Pasteur was teaching chemistry at the University of Strasbourg, he continued to study crystals. He also met Marie Laurent, the daughter of a university official. Pasteur fell in love with Marie and asked her father for her hand in marriage. Marie's father gave his permission, and the two were married in 1849.

Did you Know?

On the day before Pasteur's wedding, he went to his lab to work. He got so involved that a friend had to remind him to go to the church the next morning.

Pasteur's Notebooks

Pasteur wrote down many notes about his research. In his notebooks, he described more than 100 experiments. Many years later, the notebooks were shared with the public. Scientists have learned many things about Pasteur's work from the notes he kept.

Marie understood her husband's passion for science and his need to work nearly all the time. In the evenings, they worked together. Louis would dictate his findings, and Marie would take notes. The Pasteurs were married for 46 years and had five children.

Legion of Honor

In 1853, Pasteur was awarded the highest honor in France—the Legion of Honor. The award is given to people who provide a great service to France. The medal has five arms that represent the five degrees of the honor. Pasteur received the degree called the Grand Cross.

Pasteur met his wife and taught chemistry in Strasbourg, France.

Did You Know?

Pasteur knew that germs spread easily, so he never shook people's hands. He wouldn't even shake hands with kings and queens.

Focus on Fermentation

In 1854, at the age of 32, Pasteur and his family moved to Lille, France, where Pasteur served as dean of the Lille University of Science. Lille was an industrial city, and Pasteur hoped the science he taught would be useful in people's everyday lives.

The father of one of Pasteur's students made alcohol for a living. He was having problems with his product, so he came to Pasteur for help. He made alcohol from beet juice, using yeast to change the sugar in the juice into alcohol. This process is called fermentation. But some of his alcohol was turning sour.

Fermentation now became the focus of Pasteur's research. In his experiments, he found that both alcohol and milk contain yeast. Yeast is a tiny one-celled fungus that can grow in food. People were using certain yeasts in fermentation, but they didn't know much about it.

Pasteur worked in his laboratory nearly all the time.

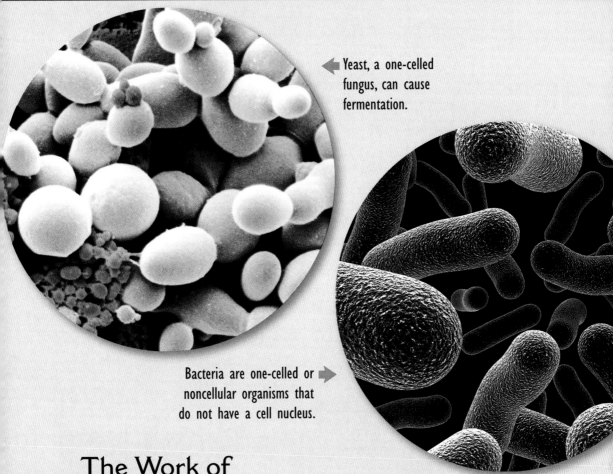

Yeast, a one-celled fungus, can cause fermentation.

Bacteria are one-celled or noncellular organisms that do not have a cell nucleus.

The Work of Microorganisms

Pasteur came up with a new theory and presented it to others. He explained that certain types of microorganisms cause fermentation. Microorganisms are tiny living things that can be seen only under a microscope. Two common types are yeast and bacteria. Yeast was causing the alcohol to ferment, but another microorganism was ruining it and turning it sour. Pasteur would soon find a way to help winemakers and save one of France's major industries.

By the age of 35, Pasteur was famous around the world. He returned to Paris, where he became director of scientific studies at the École Normale Supérieure. He had come back to the school where he had received his doctoral degree. There Pasteur continued his research on fermentation and microorganisms.

Pasteur's oldest daughter became sick with typhoid fever. At that time, people had no way to treat the disease, and his daughter died at the age of 9. Two more of his daughters also died of the disease. Some say his daughters' deaths spurred Pasteur to do more research and expand his germ theory. He wanted to find a way to protect people from disease.

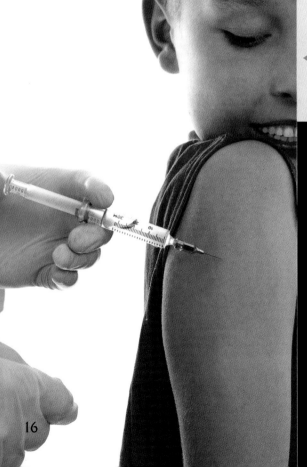

← Vaccinations protect people from getting diseases.

Typhoid Fever

Typhoid fever is a highly contagious disease caused by a bacterium called *Salmonella typhi*. The disease is transmitted through contaminated food or water. People with typhoid fever experience coughing, headaches, bleeding of the intestines, and red spots on the skin. Today there is a vaccine to prevent people from getting typhoid fever.

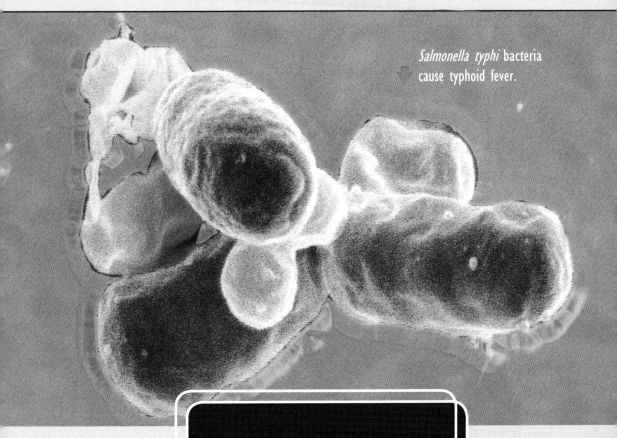

Salmonella typhi bacteria cause typhoid fever.

Tough Conditions

When Louis Pasteur took the position at the École Normale Supérieure, he didn't have a lab to work in. But he found two rooms at the school and turned them into a laboratory. The ceilings were so low he couldn't stand while he was working. He also had to crawl into the rooms on his hands and knees because the entrances were behind stairs.

Contest Winner

In the early 1800s, people believed that mold and germs developed from things that weren't living, such as rotting meat. This scientific theory was called spontaneous generation. But some scientists wanted to know if the theory was true.

In France, the Academy of Sciences, a group of professional scientists, held a contest. It would give prize money to the scientist who could prove the theory either right or wrong. Pasteur proved the theory was wrong and won the contest. He showed that food rots and develops mold only when it comes into contact with microorganisms in the air. When food is kept separate from living organisms, such as bacteria and fungi, it doesn't change.

⬆ Fungi often form furry growths on foods such as bread, grapes, and raspberries.

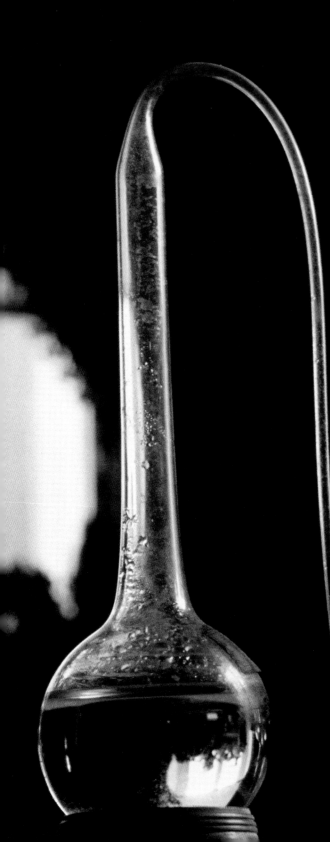

Graceful as a Swan

Swan-necked flasks with curves shaped like an "S" played an important role in Pasteur's experiments. First he boiled liquid in the flasks. Then he left them unsealed to expose them to air. Because of the shape of each flask, microorganisms were trapped in the bend of the "S" and couldn't reach the liquid. The liquid stayed pure.

◀ Swan-necked flask

Saving France's Industries

Pasteur used his findings about germs to improve France's winemaking industry. He found a certain bacterium in wine that was turning it sour. It was the same bacterium that helped create vinegar. Pasteur experimented with wine to learn how to destroy the bad bacterium.

When Pasteur heated the wine to at least 130 degrees Fahrenheit (54.4 degrees Celsius), the bacteria were destroyed. The heated wine no longer turned sour. Winemakers started heating all their wine in a process called pasteurization, named for Pasteur.

Pasteur taught beer brewers how to protect beer from bacteria by heating it to a certain temperature. Pasteur also applied his process to milk. The heat killed enough harmful organisms to extend the shelf life of milk and lengthen the time it took for it to spoil.

Then the government of France asked Pasteur to find out why silkworms were dying. The silk industry was a big business in France. Within three years, Pasteur found two diseases that were causing the problem. He was able to stop the illness from spreading, and another French industry was saved.

◄ A worker running a modern pasteurizing machine wears protective clothing so germs carried on his or her body will not contaminate the liquid.

Pasteurized Milk

Almost all milk sold today is pasteurized. It is heated to 161.6 degrees F (72 degrees C) for 15 seconds. The process kills harmful bacteria in the milk.

Silk comes from the larvae of a silkworm moth.

Silk is spun from silkworm cocoons.

Pasteur's work with wine, beer, and silkworms prepared him to study diseases that can infect animals and humans. If germs were the cause of rotten food, sour liquids, and diseased silkworms, then they could also be responsible for contagious diseases in animals and humans.

It had been nearly 20 years since the first of Pasteur's children died of typhoid fever. Pasteur wanted to know what caused their deaths. He thought harmful microorganisms were to blame, and that each disease had its own type of bacteria.

As Pasteur studied sick animals, he noticed they only had a disease once. They never got that illness again. He used this information to create vaccines that would prevent animals and humans from getting diseases. First he took the anthrax germ and weakened it. Next he injected it into healthy sheep. Even a small amount of the germ protected them from getting the disease in the future.

Pasteur also developed a vaccine for cholera, a disease that attacks the intestines and can be fatal. A bacterium called *Vibrio cholerae*, found in contaminated water or food, was to blame.

Cholera was killing off chickens by the thousands. Pasteur's vaccine was a weakened form of the bacteria that caused the disease. When Pasteur's vaccine was injected into chickens, they got sick but eventually recovered. Pasteur believed these animals were now immune to the disease— they could never get it again. Vaccinated chickens were now safe from deadly cholera.

Pasteur applied the same principle to cattle and sheep that were at risk for getting the fatal anthrax disease. His success with vaccines encouraged him to search for more ways to prevent disease. People were becoming very interested in this man who could save lives and rescue French industries.

Pasteur worked in his lab with a sterilizer.

Next Pasteur studied rabies, a deadly disease that affects the nervous system. People can catch it if an infected animal bites them. Pasteur wanted to make a vaccine that would protect animals from this disease.

Once Pasteur developed a rabies vaccine, he tested it on 50 dogs. None of them became sick when exposed to the rabies virus. Now he was asked to try his vaccine on a person. A dog with rabies had bitten a 9-year-old boy. Without help, the boy would surely die. So Pasteur tried his rabies vaccine on the boy, and the boy survived. The rabies vaccine was a success.

During the next year, more than 2,000 people were given the rabies vaccine. Today we still use the vaccine to protect animals and ourselves from the fatal disease.

Pasteur (center) was surrounded by an English doctor, nurses, and young patients who received the rabies vaccine.

Did You Know?

Pasteur made his rabies vaccine shots from the dried spinal cords of rabbits.

A doctor gave an unhappy child a vaccination in the late 1800s.

Rabies Vaccine Today

Today rabies vaccinations are given to pets to keep them from getting rabies. Veterinarians and people who work with the rabies virus are also vaccinated to protect them from the disease. Generally, people only get rabies shots if an animal suspected of having the disease has bitten them. Six shots are given over a period of 30 days. The first shot is given in the area of the bite as soon as possible after the person is bitten. The other shots are given in the arm.

Vaccines and More Vaccines

There are now vaccines for many diseases. In the United States, most children receive several vaccinations soon after birth and every so often throughout their childhood. This keeps them from getting diseases that once were common, such as diphtheria, pertussis, and tetanus. A vaccine for polio, a crippling disease, was developed and tested by Jonas Salk in 1952 and announced to the world three years later.

Starting in 1967, people worldwide were vaccinated for smallpox. The disease was virtually gone 10 years later. The chicken pox vaccine was first used in 1995.

In 1888, the Pasteur Institute opened in Paris. It began as a center for treating and studying rabies. Pasteur, the founder and director, gathered some of the brightest scientists in the world to study diseases. Together they developed ways to treat diseases such as bubonic plague, tuberculosis, diphtheria, yellow fever, and polio.

Pasteur worked at the institute until his death on September 28, 1895. He was 72 years old. He died of complications from a series of strokes that began when he was just 46. Although Pasteur was buried in the Cathedral of Notre Dame, in Paris, France, his body was later buried at the Pasteur Institute, where it lies today.

Louis Pasteur later in life

The work done by Louis Pasteur saved millions of lives during his lifetime. Today his vaccines are still protecting humans and animals from diseases. His pasteurization process saved several of France's main industries and continues to improve our everyday lives.

HIV

About 100 years after the Pasteur Institute was founded, scientists there were the first to identify HIV, the virus that causes AIDS.

The Pasteur Institute in Paris has been an important center in the fight against diseases for more than a century.

Pasteur's Legacy

Many people rank Louis Pasteur as one of the most important scientists the world has ever known. His work marked the beginning of microbiology, the study of microorganisms and how they affect other living things. His pioneering work and the lives he saved make him an important part of several fields of science: microbiology, chemistry, immunology, medicine, and more.

He is probably best known for pasteurization, since it bears his name. But his worldwide impact is largely due to his remarkable vaccines. The vaccines he developed for cholera, anthrax, smallpox, rabies, and other diseases still prevent deadly diseases in people and animals.

Pasteur started with just a theory—the idea that microorganisms, particular bacteria, are responsible for diseases. Few people believed him at the time, but he confidently researched and experimented. His ideas became the foundation of modern medicine. Pasteur set the stage for later breakthroughs in immunization and antibiotics, the medicines that can destroy or stop the growth of harmful bacteria.

We are also reminded of Pasteur's legacy whenever we open the refrigerator to get some milk. We can thank Pasteur for better health, longer lives, and the prevention of diseases that had threatened people's lives for centuries. We also remember the scientists who have learned from Pasteur and continue to carry on important work against some of the most brutal diseases ever to afflict humanity.

The Pasteur Institute

Today the Pasteur Institute is still at the forefront of scientific research. It includes nine research departments and has more than 500 researchers and 600 trainees. Eight of its scientists have been awarded the Nobel Prize for medicine or physiology. Branches of the institute can be found in many parts of the world.

Pasteur's contributions to the world he lived in and to all people for all time are astounding. His pioneering work and the lives that his work has saved make him one of the greatest scientists of all time.

Actor Paul Muni played Louis ➡ Pasteur in a 1936 movie.

Pasteur in the Movies

In 1936, a movie was made about Louis Pasteur's life. It was called *The Story of Louis Pasteur* and starred Paul Muni as Pasteur. The film won an Oscar for best screenplay, and Muni received an Oscar for best actor in a leading role.

Name:	Louis Pasteur
Date of birth:	December 27, 1822
Nationality:	French
Birthplace:	Dole, France
Parents:	Jean-Joseph Pasteur and Jeanne Roqui
Wife:	Marie Laurent
Children:	Jeanne, Jean Baptiste, Cecile, Marie Louise, Camille
Date of death:	September 28, 1895
Place of burial:	Cathedral of Notre Dame in Paris, France; later moved to the Pasteur Institute in Paris
Fields of study:	Microbiology and chemistry
Known for:	Finding causes and preventing diseases
Contributions to science:	Pasteurization and vaccines against anthrax, rabies, and other diseases
Awards and honors:	Legion of Honor; Leeuwenhoek medal
Publications:	*The Physiological Theory of Fermentation; The Germ Theory and Its Applications to Medicine and Surgery*

Ferdinand Cohn (1828–1898)
German biologist considered one of the founders of
microbiology; he classified bacteria as plants and divided
bacteria into four groups

Casimir Davaine (1812–1882)
French physician and microbiologist who discovered the
anthrax bacterium and showed how it is passed from
one animal to another

Robert Hooke (1635–1703)
English scientist credited with observing the first
cells under a microscope and naming them *cellulae*
(cells); he drew detailed images of his observations
using a microscope and published them in 1665 in
his book *Micrographia*

Robert Koch (1843–1910)
German physician who was awarded the Nobel Prize in
medicine for his discovery of the tuberculosis bacterium;
he is considered one of the founders of microbiology

Anton van Leeuwenhoek (1632–1723)
Dutch scientist who made hundreds of microscopes and
observed bacteria cells for the first time; he is commonly
known as the father of microbiology

1340s	Bubonic plague strikes Europe, killing millions of people
1414	First case of influenza is reported in France
1624	Thomas Sydenham identifies scarlet fever and measles
1647	First recorded cases of yellow fever in the Americas
1659	Typhoid fever is first described by Thomas Willis
1665	Robert Hooke views the cell structure of cork under a microscope
1683	Anton van Leeuwenhoek discovers living bacteria in pond water and on human teeth
1831	Robert Brown reports his discovery of the nucleus, the command center of the cell
1838	Matthias Schleiden finds that plants are made of cells
1844	Karl Nägeli sees the process of cell growth and division under a microscope
1850	French physician Casimir Davaine and French dermatologist Pierre François Olive Rayer discover the anthrax bacterium in the blood of diseased sheep
1855	Rudolf Virchow discovers that all living cells come from other living cells
1870	Pasteur and Robert Koch establish that certain microorganisms, or germs, are the cause of many diseases

1881	Pasteur develops a vaccine for anthrax
1882	Pasteur develops a vaccine for rabies; Koch discovers the bacterium responsible for tuberculosis, for which he receives the Nobel Prize in medicine
1888	The Pasteur Institute opens in Paris, France
1890	Emil von Behring uses antitoxins to make tetanus and diphtheria vaccines; immunology, the study of the immune system, is developed by Paul Ehrlich
1897	English physician Ronald Ross determines that a mosquito transmits the malaria parasite in humans
1921	Frederick Banting and Charles Best discover that insulin is important for the treatment of diabetes
1923	First vaccine for diphtheria is developed
1926	First vaccine for pertussis is developed
1927	First vaccine for tetanus is developed
1928	Alexander Fleming discovers penicillin, which kills bacteria and helps fight some diseases
1935	First vaccine for yellow fever is developed
1952	Jonas Salk develops the first polio vaccine

1962	First oral polio vaccine is used
1964	First vaccine for measles is developed
1967	First vaccines for mumps and smallpox are developed
1970	First vaccine for rubella is developed
1977	Smallpox virus is believed to be extinct in the world, although samples of the virus are kept in laboratories for research purposes
1981	First vaccine for hepatitis B is developed
1995	First vaccine for chicken pox is developed
2003	Carlo Urbani of Doctors Without Borders alerts the World Health Organization about the SARS (Severe Acute Respiratory System) virus, resulting in the most effective response to an epidemic in history; Urbani dies of the disease in less than a month
2007	The U.S. Food and Drug Administration approves the first vaccine for humans against the avian influenza virus H5N1
2008	U.S. Centers for Disease Control and Prevention conducts a study to find out if exposure to a preservative in vaccines in infancy is related to the development of autism

Glossary

anthrax—fatal disease caused by the bacterium *Bacillus anthracis*

antibiotics—drugs that kill bacteria and are used to cure infections and diseases

atoms—tiniest parts of an element that have all the properties of that element

bacterium—single-celled or noncellular organism that lives in soil, water, organic matter, or the bodies of plants and animals

chemistry—science of the structure and reactions of chemical elements and the compounds they form

cholera—sometimes fatal disease of the small intestine that is spread in contaminated water and food

crystals—solids formed by the solidification of a chemical and having a highly regular atomic structure

fermentation—changing sugar to carbon dioxide and alcohol through a process involving yeast

flasks—bottles with narrow necks that are used in science laboratories

fungus—plantlike organism that has no leaves, flowers, roots, or chlorophyll

infectious—capable of causing infection

larvae—insects at the stage of development between egg and pupa

microbiology—science that studies microorganisms and their effects on other living things

microorganisms—life forms that are too small to see without a microscope

microscope—instrument used to make very small objects appear larger

mold—plants that make spores instead of seeds to reproduce

molecules—smallest parts of a substance that display all the chemical properties of that substance

nucleus—central part of a cell that contains the chromosomes

pasteurization—heating a drink or other food to kill microorganisms that can cause disease, spoiling, or unwanted fermentation

rabies—deadly disease that can infect most warm-blooded animals and is passed on by the saliva of infected animals

spores—single-celled reproductive bodies that can grow into new organisms

strokes—conditions caused by a sudden lack of oxygen in part of the brain caused by the blocking or breaking of a blood vessel

tanners—people who change animal skins into leather

theory—proposed explanation of a group of facts

typhoid fever—deadly disease caused by bacteria and passed on mostly by contaminated food or water

vaccine—liquid containing weakened or dead microbes that provide immunity against a disease

yeast—one-celled fungi that can cause fermentation and are used to make wine and beer; also used to make bread rise and become light

Additional Resources

Anderson, Rodney P. *The Invisible ABCs*. Washington, D.C.: ASM Press, 2007.

Brunelle, Lynn. *Bacteria*. Milwaukee: Gareth Stevens Publishing, 2004.

Claybourne, Anna. *Microlife: From Amoebas to Viruses*. Chicago: Heinemann, 2004.

Fandel, Jennifer. *Louis Pasteur and Pasteurization*. Mankato, Minn.: Capstone Press, 2007.

Pascoe, Elaine. *Single-Celled Organisms*. New York: PowerKids Press, 2003.

On the Web

For more information on this topic, use FactHound.

1. Go to *www.facthound.com*

2. Type in this book ID: 0756539625

3. Click on the *Fetch It* button.

FactHound will find the best Web sites for you.

Index

Lisa Zamosky

Lisa Zamosky earned her master's degree from the University of Southern California and worked in the health care field in New York City for more than 10 years before becoming a freelance writer. Zamosky has written more than 40 books for the education market. She also writes articles involving scientific and medical research, covering medicine, pharmaceuticals, biotechnology, fitness, nutrition, and the health-care system for consumer and business magazines, both in print and on the Web. Zamosky lives in Southern California with her husband and son.